STREETS BROAD AND NARROW

IMAGES OF VANISHING DUBLIN

STREETS BROAD AND NARROW

IMAGES OF VANISHING DUBLIN

Kevin C. Kearns

GILL & MACMILLAN

Gill & Macmillan Ltd
Hume Avenue, Park West
Dublin 12
with associated companies throughout the world
www.gillmacmillan.ie
© Kevin C. Kearns 2000
0 7171 2861 X

Design and print origination by
O'K Graphic Design, Dublin

Printed in Malaysia

This book is typeset in 10.5/14 pt Adobe Garamond.

A CIP catalogue record for this book is available from the
British Library.

1 3 5 4 2

For Cathe, Megan, and Sean

"In the final analysis the inner city is a microcosm of Irish Society."

(Mick Rafferty, *The Urban Plunge*)

"The city centre is the heart that pumps life into the outer limbs. It is tradition. It is our past."

(Ronan Sheehan and Brendan Walsh, *The Heart of the City*)

"Every narrow street within sound of the gay bells of St Patrick's has its memories … there is life in those streets, the narrow streets where Molly Malone could have lived. (But) it is in these wide streets that modern Molly Malones push barrows loaded with flowers … yes, every street, broad and narrow, has its traditions."

(Olivia Robertson, *Dublin Phoenix*)

Echoes

He that has trod our city's streets
And has heard the tales of old …
Who but he has heard so much
That has so well been told?
And did he listen with willing ear
To ballad and rhyme and song
Then he heard an old Town's tale
In the music of the throng.

He that has heard the wild catcalls
And harked to the old nick-name …
Who but he has heard so much
Of our follies and our fame?
And did he hear, down through the years,
The doggerels that deride
Then he heard an old town's taunting
At pomposity and pride.

He that has walked the Georgian square
And the old Victorian places …
Who but he has heard so much
Of a city's airs and graces?
And did he view with knowing eye
Such elegance and charm
Then he's walked with Swift and Joyce …
And he's walked it arm-in-arm.

(Vincent Caprani)

Kevin C. Kearns PhD is a social historian and Professor Emeritus at the University of Northern Colorado. He has made thirty research trips to Ireland, a number of which have been funded by the National Geographic Society. Of his seven books on Dublin, four have been bestsellers, most notably *Dublin Tenement Life: An Oral History* and *Dublin Pub Life and Lore*. He now resides in the village of Charlotte, Vermont.

CONTENTS

Introduction   1

"Reared in a Banana Box"   8

House-proud Traditions   10

Horse-handlers   12

Reciting Yeats and Gospel   14

Pavement Playgrounds   16

Buskers and Balladeers   20

Shop-front Heritage   22

Dublin's Last Two Forges   26

Street Wagering   28

Faded Grandeur   30

Cumberland Street Dealers   32

The Art of Conversation   34

Natural Posers   36

The Local Pub—and Sanctuary   38

Neighbourhoods and Neighbouring   40

Irish Eyes and Comeliness   44

Waiting for Business   46

Traditional Corner Shops   50

"The Last Cooperage … Last of the Tribe"   52

Demolished Buildings and Broken Hearts   54

Tending the Stalls   58

Disparate Doorways   62

Travelling People in the City   64

Doorway Denizens   68

"The Salt of the Earth" in Artisans' Dwellings   70

Men of Letters   76

Flatland Kids   78

Grafton Street Theatre   82

A Swing in Mountjoy Square   84

Old-fashioned Horse-dealing   86

Chalkies   88

Rooting Around on "the Hill"   90

GRANDES DAMES—"PURE INNOCENCE"   94

SHOP WINDOW SIMPLICITY   96

CLAMOUR ON COBBLESTONES   98

PAUSING FOR A BIT OF CHAT   100

A HELPING HAND AND HEART   104

LOFTY FIDDLERS   106

WAITING ON THE SMITHY   108

SILENT STATEMENTS   110

URBAN SADDLERS   114

A GOOD SPIEL   116

TRUE PINTMEN   118

THAT OLD GANG OF MINE   120

SATURDAY BROWSING   124

"OH, THE HORSE IS DYING OUT IN DUBLIN"   126

INNER-CITY BACKLANDS   130

DERVISHES AND ACROBATS   134

ALLEYS OF INTRIGUE   136

PALS   138

DELIVERY DAY   140

ARTISTRY BENEATH ONE'S FEET   142

SCALING THE SUMMITS   144

SOLITARY SOULS   146

A PIPE IS LIKE A GOOD FRIEND   148

DIFFERENT WALKS OF LIFE   150

HORSES OF FANCY   152

WHEELING PRAMS AND HANDCARTS   154

COTTAGE SERENDIPITY   156

OLD SHOEMAKERS … "THE END OF THE LINE"   158

THE COMPANIONSHIP OF A GOOD CANE   160

"RAISING PIGS IN THE CITY IS OUTDATED"   162

CATCHING SUMMER'S SUN   166

SMITHFIELD SIDE-SHOWS   168

GOOD NEWS AND BAD   172

RELICS OF MOLLY MALONE   174

ELEGANCE IN DECAY   176

SUGGESTED READINGS   179

INTRODUCTION

The inner city has a life and spirit of its own.

(Bairbre Power, *Sunday Independent*, 1981)

Cities are often thought of in terms of their architecture, their art, their streetscapes. But the soul of any city is its people. Dublin has always been fortunate in having a rich bounty of quite extraordinary people.

(Michael Keating TD, former Lord Mayor of Dublin)

There is such a thing as Dublin spirit. It is recognised when it is met and it underlies the feeling of being distinct and valuable—the feeling of being a rare breed—which is characteristic of Dublin people. It is involved with a relish for living, love of company, love of language, humour, defiance of adversity, generosity, loyalty to friends, identification with place.

(Ronan Sheehan and Brendan Walsh)

The soul and spirit of Dublin—much alluded to, seldom captured. Ethereal, yet palpable. Seen in faces, heard in conversation, observed in behaviour. Earthy and profound. Often expressed by one human voice as well as the verbal clamour of an entire street. Alternately civil, profane, witty, defiant, gracious. Indomitably Joycean. Unabashedly provincial. Exhilarating. Exasperating. Distressingly indefinable. Yet countless individuals have endeavoured to do so with the power of language and magic of the lens. I, too, have attempted to portray the soul and spirit of Dublin's inner-city heartland in my books. But one is always left feeling that there is so much more to tell, to reveal. Perhaps it is because, as Leon Uris once opined, "Dublin is probably as much a state of mind as any place in the world."[1]

As a social historian, I began my summer research trips to Dublin in the turbulent sixties. It was a period of new prosperity and modernisation; but unbridled urban redevelopment by insensitive planners and greedy developers led to widespread physical destruction of the old cityscape. I was struck—often shocked—by the blatant obliteration of fine historic architecture. The demolition of stately Georgian streetscapes so alarmed me that I felt compelled to write a book on the subject, entitled *Georgian Dublin: Ireland's Imperilled Architectural Heritage*. Three years of research on this subject drew me into Dublin's oldest, most historic neighbourhoods, from the Liberties to the north side. I soon found that it was not just the Georgian architecture that was being ravaged. Equally conspicuous was the wanton destruction of family dwellings, local shops, pubs, entire streets and neighbourhoods, customs and traditions—a whole way of life. Especially heartbreaking was the callous uprooting of native Dubliners from their ancestral homes, to be transplanted in sterile, soulless suburban housing estates.

Being witness to historic architectural loss and human tragedy jolted my sensibilities, both as a person and as a historian. Each summer I made more inner-city friends and came to feel their anguish and frustration. Like them, I felt impotent to halt the process or even to make significant change. But as a social historian it sparked in my mind the need to at least try to record what had survived of the old inner-city life before it too had vanished. I determined that the most authentic method of documenting traditional life ways and lore was that of recording oral historical testimony from the people who had lived their lives there. With the support of several research institutions, particularly the National Geographic Society, I embarked on my personal odyssey of chronicling what remained of Dublin's tattered heartland. For thirty consecutive summers I came to Dublin, lived on the north side, met thousands of inner-city folk, and wrote seven books. The subjects of these books clearly reflect my perceptions of what needed to be recorded: tenement life, vanishing craftsmen, the old Stoneybatter neighbourhood, street life and lore, the local pub as a social institution. With each research project there was a sense of urgency, as I knew that often I was only a few strides ahead of the bulldozers, a few days in advance of evictors. I was also keenly aware that since most of my oral history respondents were between the ages of sixty-five and ninety-five, a day's delay could mean a life story lost.

My thirty summers of exploratory rambling through Dublin's cityscape was always by foot—the only way to find interviewees, get to *know* the people, *feel* the gritty fabric of their neighbourhoods. Standard research gear for such forays was a sturdy backpack stuffed with tape recorders, street maps, notebooks, pens, and collapsible umbrella. And *always* the cameras.

Cameras served as vital research instruments for visually documenting individuals and settings for a book in progress. However, from the outset of my urban trekking I possessed the foresight to pause in my daily work and photographically record a sight encountered that had some historic or intrinsic human value. This often meant dodging horses and cars, trying to simultaneously manoeuvre an open umbrella and cameras, inviting the wrath of a temperamental street dealer, or incurring jeers from wary subjects. Over these many years I took more than four thousand photographs of inner-city life and neighbourhoods. It was my lofty ambition to one day produce an unconventional photographic-historical book on Dublin's heartland. As the year 2000 approached, the time seemed perfect.

Dublin under the camera's eye

> *"Fate seems to have been especially unkind to Irish photographic history."*[2]

Photography came early to Ireland. In 1838 Daguerre perfected his invention in France, and by 1842 a Daguerrotype studio had been established in Dublin. In 1854 the Dublin Photographic Society was founded. The most renowned commercial photographer of his day was William Lawrence, whose studio was in Upper Sackville Street. He amassed a collection of nearly forty thousand plates. In the early days of photography, and up to the early years of the twentieth century, Irish photographers concentrated their efforts on scenic landscapes, on important buildings and thoroughfares, official occasions, and elite society. Since the purpose of much photography was to produce profitable postcards, it was often preferable to get photographs of scenery or buildings with "no living thing in sight."[3] Indeed people were often regarded as a nuisance or a blemish on the scene. Human images, when recorded, were customarily in crowd scenes.

Following his death in 1932 at the age of ninety-one, Lawrence's collection was fortuitously purchased by the National Library. However, a good number of plates had been destroyed in 1916 or lost through other means. Those that survived were largely landscapes and streetscapes. Regrettably, his portraits and any domestic subjects were largely missing. Collections by other Dublin photographers too often met a similar fate, being either destroyed, discarded, or simply lost.

Even as the profession of photography advanced and stretched well into the middle of this century, there tended to be a certain formality and detachment about the work of Dublin photographers. As Maurice Gorham explains:

> *"It was exceptional for the harsher side of life to find its way into the lens ... with undue emphasis certainly on the sunny side ... [only] an occasional glimpse of what was going on underneath. Irish photographers were slow to turn their attention to the seamy side ... they tended to ignore the unseemly."*[4]

Similarly, throughout much of this century it was the practice of many historians and writers to ignore the "unseemly", such as poverty, tenement life, and human failings among the masses. Historians commonly believed, as apparently did most photographers, that there was little merit in documenting the life of common people, the working class, lower-income districts, daily work patterns, street activity, and the like. It was simply thought that they held no historical importance or interest. Precious few are the photographic collections that provide glimpses of what lay underneath Dublin's proper veneer.

Against this background, and with no credentials as a professional photographer, I submit my modest contribution to Dublin's photographic history. The photographs comprising this book cover the last thirty years of this century. But what a third of a century it has been, in change and loss! As Bill Kelly wrote in the early nineteen-eighties,

> *"In the first thirty years of this century Dublin didn't change much. It changed a lot in the next thirty, and a lot more the following fifteen. The people changed, the scene changed."*[5]

Without question, the last three decades have seen the most profound physical and social transformation of Dublin's heartland: dramatic, bewildering change—an important period during which to have had a camera as constant companion.

Gorham contends that typical Dublin photographic collections include only "a few samples of intimate photographs" of normal Dubliners.[6] By contrast, this is a "grass-roots" (or concrete pavement) photographic exposition which portrays common people leading their ordinary daily lives. These black-and-white images are meant to be human and intimate. Taken individually, they may not appear historically striking, but viewed collectively I hope they create a human mosaic that reveals the soul and spirit of the inner city in all its complexity.

A photographic history needs integrity as well as authenticity. Consequently, this collection includes both the "sunny" and the "seamy"—for this is the reality of the inner-city realm. A genuine effort has been made to vary and balance subject matter in a representative manner. Those who know the city over the past third of a century will recognise the distressing sights: dereliction, decay, faded Georgian grandeur, grim flats, poverty areas, disadvantaged children. Such sights are common in large urban centres. To omit them here would be manipulative, dishonest. They are more than counterbalanced by the myriad positive images depicting daily heartland life: hordes of frolicking children, gregarious adults, colourful market dealers, dignified "old crowd", neighbourhood traditions, and exuberant street life.

In essence, this book is about people, for, as Michael Keating rightly declares, "the soul of any city is its people." To historically enrich and socially enliven the book, quotations and oral history testimonies accompany many of the photographs. They may reveal thoughts and emotions behind facial expressions, or give voice to the human condition in the inner city. While the photographs cover the last third of the century, the oral narratives sometimes take us back to the first third, thereby giving a sense of continuity to city life.

Focusing the lens

Dublin has always been a colourful patchwork of neighbourhoods. While too many have been eradicated by urban renewal, a good many remain intact. The old neighbourhoods, arranged in rows or terraces, were built on a human scale that creates a natural harmony between people and their houses and neighbours. They form close-knit communities highly conducive to the traditional custom of neighbouring. Residents born and reared along the street can trace their family back generations and have known their neighbours since childhood. They share common roots, heritage, pride in place. Sharing and caring for one another is an age-old custom. It's just their "nature" to look after one another. In the inner city, being a bona-fide "good neighbour" is one of the highest accolades bestowed. Indeed, neighbourly relations can be nearly as strong as family ties.

It is not mere cliché to say that inner-city natives are a different breed, within a separate culture from their suburban counterparts. Because they possess their own history and lifeways—as well as problems and challenges—their entire life experience has been profoundly different from that of Dubliners reared elsewhere. Despite their often disadvantaged status, they have a fierce pride in their urban homeland. Many outsiders couldn't begin to comprehend their powerful attachment to family dwelling, street, neighbourhood, local church, shop, and pub. It is emotionally and psychologically part of their very being. This is their ancestral ground. Being an inner-city person is a source of great pride, like being of pioneer stock. "My grandparents were from this street" is a mighty boast in these parts. For many it would be unthinkable—almost a betrayal—to willingly leave the area of their forebears. Outsiders who may pity their inner-city brethren for living in what they might regard as "no-go" areas might find it unfathomable to learn that, given the choice, most would have no desire to resettle in the posh, upwardly mobile suburbs. As Leslie Foy, born and reared in Kirwan Street in old Stoneybatter, simply vouches, "I was born in this house. I know who my people were. It's something that's part of you. I belong here."

Most neighbourhoods are teeming with children. They are the essential ingredient of what urban sociologists term "living streets", necessary for the health of any city. Streets, alleys and pavements are their playgrounds. Like their parents before them, they scramble about playing football, handball, relieve-o, marbles, hopscotch, penny toss. Full of devilment, they still jeer "oul fellas", dash wildly through traffic, swing precariously on lamp-posts. Their hollering and laughter resonate pleasingly through bricked corridors. As Pete St John observes, there is something different about a "child of the inner city"—a resourcefulness, independence, toughness necessary to survive.[7] To be sure, they face hazards little known earlier in the century, such as dangerous traffic, pollution, crime, drugs, and assorted harmful temptations. Yet they exude boundless energy and positive spirit, which bring joyful animation to the streets, enlivening the adult world around them. Often, in the "greyness" that sometimes prevails, children seem like the bright flowers of the inner city.

The older neighbourhoods are also notable for the legions of elderly, known affectionately as the "old crowd" or "old stock". Most grew up in tenements or artisans' dwellings and knew dire hardship, if not outright poverty. The oldest lived under British rule, witnessed a revolution, and survived the Great Depression. They are the visible and audible link with the past, extolling the old-type religion, morality, and family values. It has not been easy adapting to modern, frenetic Dublin. Attitudes towards city life today vary from wonder to genuine worry and despair. Disenchantment stems from the materialism, crime, and family disintegration. As 92-year-old May Hanaphy, born and reared in the most wretched tenements in Golden Lane in the Liberties, quietly confides, "Oh, I'm living on a different planet now." Yet despite the struggles of their early life, it is hard to find one among the flock who would confess a willingness to exchange childhoods with today's youngsters. In an age when such qualities are conspicuously less in evidence, they exhibit civility, dignity, and gentility. And the grand old Dublin wit. A cluster of old cronies with pension cheques in hand at week's end can still produce better wit and dialogue than most written for characters on the Abbey stage.

Capturing the street life

> "Think of a city and what comes to mind? Its streets. If a city's streets look interesting, the city looks interesting; if they look dull, the city looks dull. Streets and their side-walks, the main public places of a city, are the most vital organs."[8]

Nowhere are Dublin's soul and spirit more in evidence than in the street life. It is precisely for this reason that so many of the photographs in this book are of street figures and activities. Dublin has for centuries been famed for its exuberant street life, a fact duly noted by many early visitors in their writings. Sidney Davies, writing about *Dublin Types* some eighty years ago, termed this the "free pageant of the streets."[9] He marvelled at how Dubliners delighted in watching one another. No less true today, the streets still hold great human fascination, aswirl with motion, colour, sound, scents. Spontaneity. Unpredictability—radiating Dublin spirit. Certain streets, such as Meath Street, Thomas Street, Moore Street, Grafton Street, and Henry Street are grandiose stages for sundry human expression. And Dublin boasts a marvellous cast of interesting street types: market dealers, busking musicians, evangelists, pavement artists, poets, flower-sellers, spielers, and mimes—not to mention the naturally entertaining performers and buffoons from the ranks of the common citizenry. Especially at week's end, the city streets sparkle with human interaction and energy, creating a discernible mood of merriment. Suburbanites readily confess to venturing into the inner city to get an invigorating dose of the street soul and spirit.

Dublin's quintessential street figure is that of the mythical Molly Malone, hawking cockles and mussels through "streets broad and narrow." The city's dealers are legendary in lore and song. Perhaps the true soul and spirit of the inner city are most poignantly personified in the weathered faces of the dealers. As a 1985 editorial in the *Irish Times* proclaimed, "street traders are a part of Dublin heritage and tradition. Can any

Dubliners imagine the city without 'the dealers'?" Many were reared in a banana box beside their mother's stall. "It's just tradition … generation follows generation," they like to say. With their famous Dublin wit, tart tongues, and flamboyant personalities, they comprise one of the city's great cultural treasures. But it should be remembered that they have also played an important historical role in the life of the city. In earlier times, up to just a few decades ago, when many Dubliners were struggling with hardship, it was the dealers who saw them through. Countless poor and lower-income families were fed and outfitted at markets such as Moore Street, the Daisy Market and Iveagh Market, Cumberland Street, and Thomas Street. Apart from food, the dealers sold mountains of second-hand clothing, shoes, pots and pans, furniture, rosaries—all the necessities of life.

The halcyon days of market dealing are now a thing of the past, though it is heartening to see what has survived. It was especially sad to witness the demise of the famed Daisy Market and Iveagh Market dealers, who held out until the nineteen-nineties. As Daisy Market dealer, Annie Ryan, prophesied: "We're the last of the flock … The market is going to disappear, and we'll disappear with it." With the passing of the markets and dealers, their photographic record becomes all the more historically valuable.

People labouring hard with hands and back have always been a natural sight in the heart of Dublin. There is something humanly satisfying about watching people going about their manual occupations in the open street or at a shop bench. But in an age of mechanisation and computerisation, such sights have largely faded away. Gone are the days when one could watch, and engage in conversation, a lamplighter, docker, or coal-seller. However, a number of old trades and crafts have survived and are most enjoyable to observe. Some examples are shoemakers, stone-carvers, farriers, carters, saddlers, horse-dealers, small grocers, and butchers. There is something especially fascinating about watching a person practising an ancient trade with dated tools in hand and a serenity about the task. Only in the inner city can one peer through the clouded window of an antediluvian workshop and study an elderly craftsman hunched over his bench, plying a craft passed down from the days of the guilds. Those captured in this book have dwindled to a handful, and now their days too are numbered.

Smithfield horse fair merits special attention, because of its marvellous anachronistic character. In the first half of the twentieth century no other European capital was more dependent on horse power for its daily functioning. Firms such as Guinness, CIE, coal merchants, bakeries and dairies all used horses by the thousand. Surprisingly, a good few were still used in the sixties and seventies. Mass motorisation has now nearly driven the horse from sight. The sound of hooves on pavement, once so familiar to Dubliners, today stirs curiosity and nostalgia. Smithfield horse fair, held on the first Sunday of each month, is now a rare cultural sight, an authentic relic of an earlier epoch. The sharp clatter of hooves on the cobblestones and the pungent odour of fresh horse dung are strongly evocative of real old Dublin. The fair draws a fascinating conglomeration of old horsemen, traders, drovers, travellers, and gnarled Dublin characters. Curious onlookers savour the chiselled faces, earthy lingo, witticisms, and animated haggling over price. The frenzy and raucous nature of the event create high excitement. And when bareback riders race their horses precariously through the crowd, real drama is created. No other event in the inner city so tangibly hearkens back to the old days. But now Smithfield too is threatened by road-widening and office-building. Soon the hooves will be heard no more. Then only photographs will tell the tale.

The photographs selected for inclusion in this book are arranged in groups and mini-groups that exhibit some historical or human interest. Subjects range from the market dealers, horse-traders and street buskers to Dublin's last cooperage, forges, and shoemakers; children and teenagers playing, fighting, climbing, street gambling, "hanging out." Some photographs draw attention to often-missed sights, such as artistic coal-hole covers, elegantly decaying eighteenth-century ironwork, stone cottages, and traditional shop windows. Many images depict the most simple human moments frozen in time: figures engaged in satisfying chat, rooting around a street market, visiting a neighbour, knitting at a sunlit doorway, or enjoying the company of a good pipe—the most ordinary daily acts. But, as every Dubliner knows, they are part and parcel of the city scene. They are the small, delicate brushstrokes on the larger urban canvas. Sometimes such pictures hold our attention the longest.

In an effort to portray the holistic cityscape, included are photographs that might appear "unseemly" to some: architectural destruction and decay, economic blight, poverty, life in barren flats. But, as previously noted, these sights are characteristic of most cities. They are symptoms and symbols of urban change and socio-economic needs. They represent problems awaiting solutions; and they *need* to be part of the photographic record of the times.

It is hoped that this photographic collection will convey for future generations a historically accurate visual record of Dublin inner-city life in the last third of the twentieth century. That it will show human intimacy. That it will have captured in some significant way the unique soul and spirit of Dublin's heartland. If so, it will be a tribute to inner-city folk and a celebration of their life and heritage.

NOTES

1. Leon Uris, *Ireland: A Terrible Beauty*, New York: Doubleday 1975, 86.

2. Gorham, *Ireland Yesterday*, 5.

3. Gorham, *Ireland Yesterday*, 4.

4. Gorham, *Ireland Yesterday*, 1–4.

5. Kelly, *Me Darlin' Dublin's Dead and Gone*, 23.

6. Gorham, *Dublin Yesterday*, 5.

7. Pete St John, *Jaysus Wept!*, Birr: Midland Tribune 1984, 12.

8. Jane Jacob, *The Death and Life of Great American Cities*, New York: Random House 1961, 35.

9. Davies, *Dublin Types*, x.

Nanny Farrell,
Daisy Market dealer

"But it is Moore Street that sweet Molly Malone surely haunts, if haunt she must ... the long line of Moore Street like a gorge richly glowing with flowers and fruit. Molly Malones are sitting there by the scores, laughing and haggling, selling oranges and fresh lettuces and anemones the colour of the evening sky. As is right with such a feminine-controlled market, Moore Street has a queen."

(Olivia Robertson)

*"Rosie up in Moore Street
Tipplin' 'neath her shawl
The oul ball of malt
And the chaser
Rosie was the queen of the whole Dublin scene
When Rosie was the dealers' darlin' ..."*

(Pete St John)

"The street traders sell fruit, flowers and vegetables along the edge of the footpath, to the accompaniment of backchat, wisecracks, and many a verbal battle."

(G. Ivan Morris)

"My mother was a trader before me, and me grandmother. All of us on this street were reared in a basket—or a banana box. We all followed the trade. Oh, it's in the blood, definitely. I'd come out and help me mother. I done that for love. The thirties were hard times here. And there was one trader here had twenty-one children. Me own mother had fifteen. And, I'll tell you, the women here long ago were fine, big women. "

(Lizzy Byrne, Moore Street dealer)

Moore Street dealers

"You'd see house-proud touches: old ladies polishing the door knockers and numbers on the door and polishing the windows. And I remember seeing women, they'd sweep a whole area of the street and then light a little fire of all the rubbish. And on a Friday night women would scrub the footpath outside their house with a deck scrubber and water and Vim."

(Thomas Linehan)

"The old stock of people kept their houses up. Putting money into their house has been their pride and joy. Doors used to be dark green, brown, and red. There are some doors that could have thirty or forty layers of paint."

(Joseph Treacy)

"People always tended to be very house-proud. That was a tradition. There's always been a high degree of upkeep and maintenance. People have always been very conscious of the appearance of houses—not just their own but the whole row of houses. I can remember as a boy that Tuesday was always the day that women came out and scrubbed their paths and sills."

(Éamonn O'Brien)

"The business goes back four generations in the family. I started at thirteen. We got horses at fairs all over Ireland. We kept two hundred horses at the stables in Queen Street. We supplied Guinness's, the bakeries, a lot of dairies. And you *had to know horses.* We never had a vet—and we knew more than a vet knew."

(Pat Cooper, horse-dealer)

Smithfield

"I lived in Queen Street, with the Haymarket and Smithfield. We'd play at skipping, ring-a-rosy, and making swings on lampposts. But when the horses got loose they'd run down the street, and everyone had to clear out of the way. Go mad, the horses would. In Queen Street there was an old lady in the shop and she was sitting behind the counter and the horse came through the window and everything went out into the street. And the horse had to be shot there. He was all cut, his head. Couldn't be saved."

(Mary Roche)

Smithfield

Pat Tierney, street poet

"I wanted to see if I could revive the bardic tradition, this idea of a travelling poet. So I decided I wanted to bring poetry to the streets of Dublin. Bringing literature to the common people, that's my contribution. Bringing poetry to the streets—the works of great Irish poets. I ended up in Grafton Street. It was ideal for reciting poetry. I was looked on for the first couple of months with a mixture of curiosity and amusement. I soon broke the barriers and crowds began to gather to hear me recite from memory the poems of W. B. Yeats and Pearse. I find that I'm close to God when I read a poem. And I can actually see people on the street trying to choke back a tear."

(Pat Tierney, street poet)

Evangelist in Cumberland Street

"We were never short of entertainment, especially on the street. Almost every evening evangelical preachers provided hymn-singing sessions and delivered spine-chilling sermons on the hellish consequences of over-indulgence in the demon alcohol."

(Máirín Johnston)

"Now that the evenings are long and bright again, the children are out in force in Dublin's streets. The skipping ropes and marbles have come out of their winter storage, the hop-scotch courses and home-made swings abound, as the children turn the streets where they live into one huge playground. Children have played in the streets since streets began, on mud and sand surfaces, on cobbles and rough stones, and now on cement and tarmacadam. Streets make almost ideal playgrounds, full of things to climb on, pavements to draw on, pedestrians to jeer at, and that constant element of danger that spices all the best-loved children's games."

(Maev Kennedy, *Irish Times*, 1978)

"There was very little for children then. But you could go around and pick up bricks and build a house and get bricks and make a chair or table and put paper on it. And maybe you'd have a brick for a doll—you know, make a doll out of a brick, get a bit of coloured paper and put it around it for a bonnet. Another thing we used to do as kids was bring down potatoes and a stick and maybe a bit of coal and we'd light a fire in an old house and make a stew, maybe in a tin can that we'd find—peel it and put in the water and boil it. And half raw it used to be eaten!"

(Nancy Cullen)

"The street called ... all the knowledge in the world was nothing compared to the excitement of street games—football, marbles, conkers, beds, tops, exploring, chasing. The tug of war between my parents and the lure of the street continued for years."

(Tom McDonagh)

"Children all played in the streets, the best of games—skipping, marbles, tapping tin cans around with a stick, and ball against the wall. There was no vandalism, and the respect we had for old people was unbelievable. Young boys, they'd curse if they got mad, but they'd go 'Shh' if a woman came by. They'd have that much respect. But when I think now of the language they use in front of women!"

(Mary Bolton)

"What a strange company, these ballad makers and ballad singers! Some of them claimed to have been inspired by the fairies!"

(P. J. McCall, 1945)

Paddy "Bones" Sweeney, busker

"We probably had some kind of [street] music every day, and I can recall 'Johnny the Whistle' who produced marvellous music out of a simple tin whistle. After the 1914–18 war a number of returned soldiers who were not too badly wounded entertained us with cornet solos, and there were the assorted vocalists who kept us up-to-date with the popular songs of the day. "

(J. Nolan)

"Busking is the same as getting up on a stage. The crowd is all around facing you and you're not only singing and playing but you crack a joke or two. In the winter your hands are freezing, your back is cold, and the wind is blowing—but you've got to make money. Dublin is a good city for busking, especially the north side. Among the working people you have much better rapport."

(Frank Quinlan, busker)

"They all know me name in Dublin. Some say, 'You're the best in Dublin that we've ever heard.' When people gather around it's a form of appreciation. Ah, I've had forty or fifty people around me. To be a *real* busker you've got to face a lot of hardships. And you've got to have character: you're a *showman*, an entertainer. There's only a few of us old-timers left. It's been a beautiful way of life. "

(Paddy "Bones" Sweeney, busker)

"The traditional Irish small shop is a significant item of folk architecture. The earliest shops were open-fronted, having a counter between the shop and the street. Up to the later eighteenth century shops had no number and were identified by hanging signs. Shop fronts make their most individual and vital contribution to the street scene in the art of hand-painted lettering by a local craftsman. The once bountiful heritage of this small-scale architecture is now drastically reduced."

(Seán Rothery)

"In a way, a shopkeeper would be looked on as a kind of doctor or priest. Maybe not quite as important, but somebody they've seen there for years and know they can confide in. They've seen you and your father before you and maybe your grandfather as well. They come in and have a chat and know that what they tell you won't go any further than that."

(Noel Lynch, small grocer)

William Walshe—North King Street

Forge in Pleasants Lane

James Harding, farrier

"I was striking at the anvil at twelve years of age. I started at five shillings a week. It's tough, laborious work. You sweat a lot and you get kicked around. I have people coming around now and they look in amazement. 'What's this place?' they ask. And I say it's a forge, and they think they're going back into the eighteenth century. When I go there'll be no more. When I go in for a drink they say, 'Ah, there's yer man Jim, he's the last of the farriers in Dublin' ... and I say to myself, 'So I am.'"

(James Harding, farrier)

"When my father died he left me this forge. Back in the nineteen-forties I'm sure there would have been fifty forges in the city. The horse drew everything: groceries, turf, milk, bread, coal, laundry. The forge was a good meeting place for the chat and the crack and the fun. Men, they'd congregate in the forge, telling a few stories, even if they were lies. In winter we had big roaring fires and always these big teapots, which were as black as soot. There was always tea in a forge."

(John Boyne, farrier)

John Boyne, farrier, in his forge in Pearse Street

Seán MacDermott Street

"You started gambling at about six, pitching up to the wall with your ha'pennies and pennies. Then you graduated to different kinds of card games, the likes of don and poker, which involved you in more money. It led to stealing off the mantelpiece, where your mother'd leave money. Oh, it passed the time. Mostly we played on the street corners under the gas lamps, where you could watch for the police."

(Stephen Mooney)

Henrietta Street

"Ambling along a Georgian street is rather like entering a magical time-warp—listen and you'll hear the murmur of ghosts ... the soft and poignant clamour of the past. And in the air when you're passing by you'll hear the gentle heartbeat of yesterday. You might also hear the ghostly tinkle of a piano from some musical evening long ago when, in a street like this, Dublin was an elegant lady and every evening was enchanted."

(Aodhán Madden)

"With the men jobless, it fell to the lioness of the pride to provide for the large brood ... The street dealers went out in the morning like a cheerful gaggle of geese, and only too often trailed miserably home at night, soaked, cold and hungry. The indestructible women of the Pale, who lost the roses on their cheeks and paled only too soon."

(Lar Redmond)

"The small traders in the poorer parts of Dublin are almost invariably 'characters'. They are often quite as temperamental as the most pampered geniuses."

(Sidney Davies)

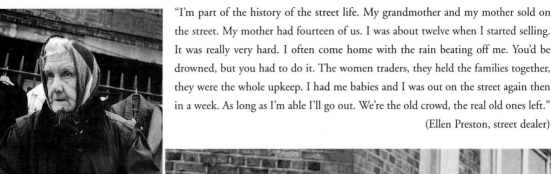

"I'm part of the history of the street life. My grandmother and my mother sold on the street. My mother had fourteen of us. I was about twelve when I started selling. It was really very hard. I often come home with the rain beating off me. You'd be drowned, but you had to do it. The women traders, they held the families together, they were the whole upkeep. I had me babies and I was out on the street again then in a week. As long as I'm able I'll go out. We're the old crowd, the real old ones left."

(Ellen Preston, street dealer)

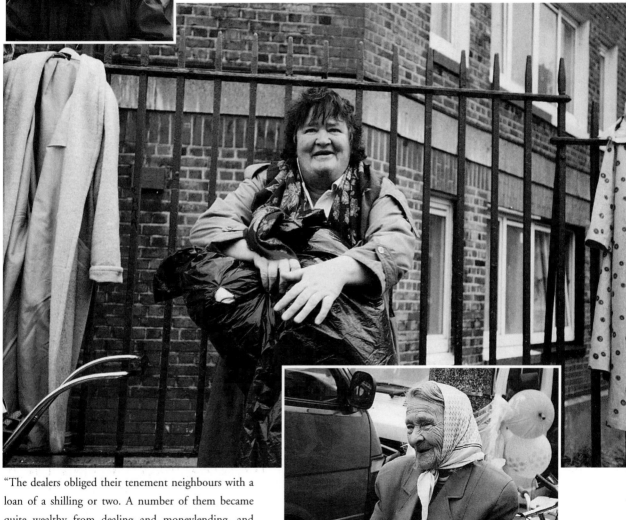

"The dealers obliged their tenement neighbours with a loan of a shilling or two. A number of them became quite wealthy from dealing and moneylending, and there's more than one doctor or lawyer or professional man today who doesn't want to trace the family tree back to his grandmother."

(Bill Kelly)

"We are the greatest talkers since the Greeks."

(Oscar Wilde)

"In Dublin, conversation is still considered an art ... Dubliners do not tell stories, they dramatise them."

(Richard M. Kain)

"Dublin is a city of individuals who glory in talk. Ordinary city noises are drowned out by the chat and laughter as the day's work is postponed for the lilting sound of talk—talk of sports, weather, horses, politics, gossip, you name it."

(Jill Uris)

"People stop and talk to each other, maybe not too worried whether they get to work on time. Indeed, one suspects quite a few do not make it at all."

(Tom Corkery)

"Talking is a favourite pastime among Dubliners in every walk of life, and no matter what he or she might be doing, it is a rare Dub who can't spend the time for gossip, speechifying, jokes, bitchery, debate, the swopping of boasts and insults and/or endless pontification about the meaning of it all."

(Katie Donovan)

"The silk-scarved politicians who have represented areas like central Dublin and have for many decades ignored the plight of so many of its children are, in my view, the real criminals."

(Tony Gregory)

"This realm of grimy cobbles and graffiti-stained walls has the look of a hard training-ground; yet the faces of its young inhabitants, combining innocence with worldly wisdom, suggest not so much the hardship of city life as the resilience and charm of Dubliners in the making."

(Brendan Lehane)

"The north inner city shows all the signs of urban decay and it has high unemployment, a landscape which has all the appearance of neglect and abandonment. The young are the most vulnerable. In a very real sense, the fact that they are born in the area limits their growth."

(Mick Rafferty)

Parnell Street

"There is more companionship in a
Dublin pub than any 'togetherness'
that Madison Avenue has dreamed of."
(Richard M. Kain)

Fownes Street

"All pubs have one thing in common.
Every one is somebody's local. Every one
has its regular customers."
(Maurice Gorham)

Aungier Street

"The pub is the centre of their life, and *every* day they're there, as regular as clockwork. Oh, the local is *their* pub. In their mind, it is their pub, and daren't you interfere with it."

(Larry Ryan, publican)

"You *stuck* to your local. That was the way it was. You made one pub your local and you were part of the furniture then. That was *our* local. I often drank twenty-two pints, in two sessions. I seen men in our pub from ten in the morning till nearly twelve at night—and they'd walk out of the pub like they never had a drink."

(John Joe Kennedy)

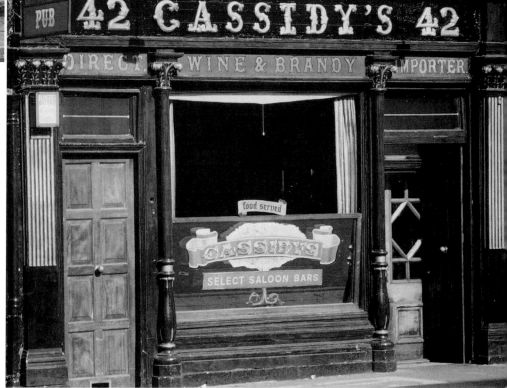

Camden Street

"Your acceptance in the local was in Dublin a saviour. A sanctuary. Beyond explaining. Here men knew their place in life. Their values as human beings."

(Pete St John)

"Ordinary, decent people understand the value of neighbourliness and had an instinctive 'sense of community' before the sociologists invented the term."

(Bertie Ahern TD, Minister for Finance)

"You'll notice that there is still a certain neighbourliness. Any afternoon you'll see people standing at their doors and talking in groups, and it's nice to see this. You'll find the ladies out with their aprons on and the hall doors wide open, and two or three from across the road would come over for a chat there on the footpath."

(Father Brendan Lawless)

"They were great neighbours. These people, they *helped* each other. The saying was, 'You can live without your relations, but you can't live without your neighbours.'"

(Father Michael Reidy)

"The ties of kinship and of neighbourhood that bind families together remain important in Dublin. For aid in times of crisis, kinship in Dublin is still a reliable bastion for the family. And relations between families living in the same neighbourhood continue to be a significant source of support in Dublin."

(Alexander J. Humphreys)

"People back then were very self-contained. They *didn't know* Dublin beyond their own environment. And they were all married around: like somebody in Foley Street was married and had a flat in Seán MacDermott Street. See, they were all interwoven. They had great community, great fun, great humour. They had a *dignity* and a pride."

(Peggy Pigott)

"Among the people themselves there existed the most genuine support and neighbourly assistance. We lived in each other's ears. We depended upon each other for the 'lend of the loan' of a cup of sugar, an egg, a few teaspoons of tea. We loaned each other clothes to go to Mass or to go looking for a job. To say that a person was 'a dacent poor skin' was the highest praise, and the most charitable person of all was the one who would 'give you the spit out of his or her mouth'."

(Máirín Johnston)

"Living on the edge of the Liberties, I had plenty of time to observe it at close quarters. There was a great sense of belonging to a close-knit community that I have never found in suburbia."

(Lar Redmond)

"Dublin is famed for the complexions of its women-folk, old as well as young; the colouring of some of the children is simply exquisite. And how fascinating the eyes that gaze so full of wonder and curiosity at the passer-by. Irish eyes are world-famed, and Dublin shows her share. Is there any city in the world that has so many pretty children as are to be seen in Dublin? Little creatures blessed with the great gift of comeliness ... undoubted beauties in the making."

(A. Peter, 1925)

"It was in 1934 that Broadstone playground opened ... an American friend had an elaborate camera with which to take photographs of the children. She aimed her camera at two children charmingly craned round a drinking fountain—'they just grin at me!' Sure enough, the two children, by some instinct, had swung round facing the camera with wide smiles ... (as) the resigned press photographers would merely take a panoramic view of a sea of smiles. The children were living up to the reputation of 'The Smiling Irish'."

(Olivia Robertson)

St Stephen's Green

Luana Cullen Tannan, North King Street

"This was my grandfather's shop, and I'm eighty now. This was a grocery and provisions shop. We sold oats, Indian meal, and bran and flake meal, and there'd be ponies and carts outside the shop. I still have two bins there now, for bran for horses and animals. I'm the last shop still selling grains loose. I was behind the counter when I was two ... it's been my life."

(Luana Cullen Tannan)

"My father was a jarvey and back to me grandfather. A jarvey was a sort of handed-down job. I started in 1923. We had a hazard at the North Wall where the Holyhead boat come in. And then you had the railways and O'Connell Street. There was enough jarveys—*hundreds*. Most of us wore a soft hat or a bowler hat and a tie. There was some fine vehicles, a hackney car and cabs like a carriage. Men took pride in their vehicles, and you had silver and brass harness. The horse was the main ingredient in the game and you had to look after him. And you'd talk to him. I think that's what made a good horseman, talking to the horse. The horse, he was *one of the family*!"

(Johnny Rearden, jarvey)

Smithfield

Jimmy Byrne, North King Street

"People used to go around collecting with these big basket prams made out of cane with a wooden handle and two wheels and a wheel in front. They'd bring in old sacks of rags and bottles. We got everything ... we got some antique stuff in. And I used to break up lovely brass beds. Ah, today you could get five hundred quid for a brass bed. There's no rags or bottles now. It's brass, copper, old washbasins, toilets, prams and doors and that. I still struggle through life. But I reared seven children. If you're happy in the old place it's all right."

(Jimmy Byrne, collector)

Cumberland Street

Smithfield

Sitric Road

"The sweet shop has always been a gathering point for people. Some people have been coming in here every morning for the past thirty years to buy their newspaper or cigarettes. You could nearly set your clock by it. In many ways we're sort of confessors for customers."

(Pat Moylett, sweet shop owner)

Sitric Road

"Time is running out for the little corner shops."

(Deirdre Kelly)

Red Cow Lane and North King Street

"The corner shop, in the days when we were very young, assumed to our eyes the proportions of a department store. It was the hub of our universe. Nowhere in the whole wide world was there anything to compare with it. The little neighbourhood shops of Dublin re-echoed the heartbeat of the city. Supplying everything from a packet of starch to a stick of 'peggy leg', they were also meeting places and gossip exchanges. On Sundays the shop at the corner knew its finest hour, for then we flocked to it in a horde to spend the traditional 'Sunday penny', a passport to most of the treasures in cardboard boxes in that small window."

(John J. Dunne)

"My name it is Seán Dempsey, as Dublin as can be,
Born hard and late in Pimlico in a house that ceased to be.
By trade I was a cooper, lost out to redundancy,
Like my house that fell to progress, my trade to memory."

(From "Dublin in the Rare Ould Times")

"I'm not making any money at it, but I want to hold on. It's sad, isn't it? Back when I first started it was really a great craft. The money was good. They were great times. You worked hard, you got great satisfaction out of completing a wood barrel, having something that's lasting. I'm the last cooper doing coopering now. When I die the craft will die with me ... I'm the last of the tribe."

(Robert Dunne, cooper)

Robert Dunne, cooper

Dunne's Cooperage, Smithfield

"I've heard it said that we Dunne's are the second-oldest name in the Coopers' Society. I'm sure it goes back to the fifteen-hundreds. I love the place. I've been coming in here so long that I couldn't sell it. But in another ten years Smithfield will be gone, this place'll be gone. This is the last cooperage. It'll soon be gone for all time. It'll just survive in history books ... I'm the very end of the line."

(Eddie Dunne, cooper)

Mountjoy Square

St Paul's Street

"People, in a sense, are embodied in buildings. Their houses, their shops, pubs, churches, which are the heart and soul of a living community, giving it identity and stability. Therefore, to upset people and lay waste to their community for road-widening or office blocks is to deprive people of part of themselves. It is a sin against the people. It is a breaking of people's hearts."

(Victor Griffin)

Harcourt Street

"The eyesores are everywhere—weed-strewn derelict sites surrounded by decaying hoardings, dilapidated buildings boarded up and left to face the elements, and gap-toothed streets."

(Frank McDonald)

North Great George's Street

Seán MacDermott Street

"They tear down a street and put the people out. Uprooted people. Put them out in Coolock, in Tallaght, Crumlin, Ballyfermot. Moved them out. That's what happened to so many Dublin people. They died of broken hearts. They just gave up. They vegetated. Their hearts never left Seán MacDermott Street, Marlborough Street, where their houses were ripped down. People's hearts are dying."

(Leslie Foy)

"Most of those areas like Dominick Street are all gone now. And along Parnell Street, it's gone. Completely gone now. They were all moved out to places like Ballyfermot and Finglas, and it changed the heart of Dublin. And *none* of them wanted to go. I suppose anyone who has been torn up from their roots, it's a very sad experience. And it was funny, you could move a man ten miles out and on a Saturday night he'd come back into the old pub for his drink."

(Paddy Casey, garda)

St Paul's Street

"I was born here in St Paul's Street, a lovely street. Seventy-six families. Like a little community. These houses are nearly a hundred years old. When I cam home from work one night and saw the bulldozers I was shocked. We should have been notified they were going to demolish the street. Houses came down like a ton of bricks. You've lived all your life on this street. The *anger* is to see the way they've knocked it down and put out genuine tenants. The rubble, it's just like Belfast, like a bombed-out place. It makes you want to scream. It'll be sad to leave the street. There'll be tears. I'll keep coming back."

(Bridge McDonagh)

"I'm angry at the devastation of my native city. I'm angry at the featureless monstrosities that are arising from the well-loved streets, and I'm angry for the city-dwellers who are forced to live in anonymous suburban dormitories. I could weep."

(Father Paul Freeney)

Thomas Street

Lizzy Byrne, Moore Street dealer

Iveagh Market

"There were thirteen children, and my mother was a tugger and used to go all over with a basket car. Knocked at doors and bought clothes, shoes, odd household goods, anything she'd see a few bob in. I used to stand and sell with her when I was about eight. It was great here in the old days. The market would be packed. Every stall was full. You could find anything you wanted in here, everything. It got people through the hard times. The Iveagh Market, it has an awful lot of historical significance, but it's nearly finished."

(Ida Lahiffe, Iveagh Market dealer)

Kathleen Maguire,
Daisy Market dealer

"You will find the charm of this tucked-away shopping venue of Dublin, this quaint, old-world, happy-go-lucky corner of the city that they call the Daisy Market. Far from the fashionable department stores, there is romance in its very name. You will find the random barrows and stands and stalls a wonderland of adventure. It is casual and human and generous, this Daisy Market. Through changing years it has remained unchanged, tucked away out of sight, one of those quaint surprise spots so characteristic of the real Dublin."

(John J. Dunne)

Moore Street

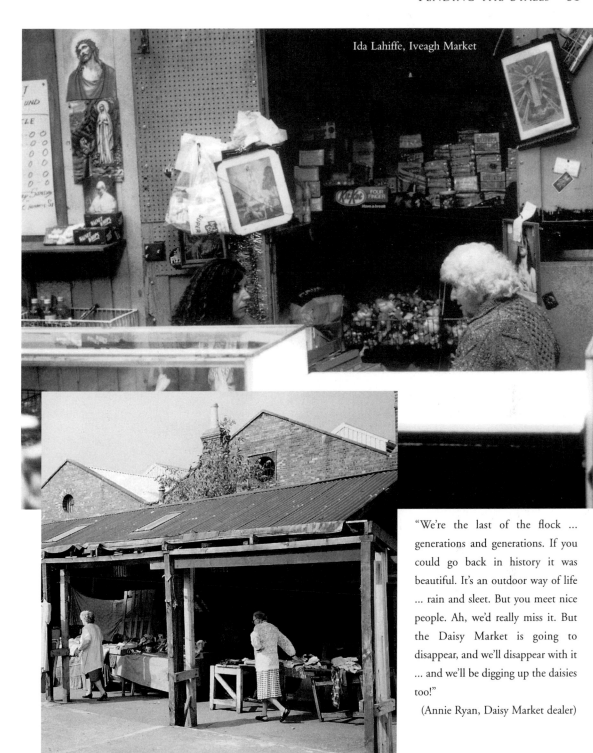

Ida Lahiffe, Iveagh Market

Daisy Market

"We're the last of the flock ... generations and generations. If you could go back in history it was beautiful. It's an outdoor way of life ... rain and sleet. But you meet nice people. Ah, we'd really miss it. But the Daisy Market is going to disappear, and we'll disappear with it ... and we'll be digging up the daisies too!"

(Annie Ryan, Daisy Market dealer)

"As everybody knows, the Dublin style of street architecture is plain to the point of severity. Except for the doorways. In the treatment of doorways, variety and individuality come into their own."

(Maurice Craig)

"Tinker camps may differ in detail but the first impressions are always the same: sounds of barking dogs and neighing horses mingle with the smells of boiled cabbage and wood smoke from the camps of squat canvas tents and caravans. A swarm of muddy children gather around ... women appear at doorways and from beneath tent flaps and gaze with silent suspicion at the intruder."

(Janine Wiedel)

"We were the travelling people, so I was from all over Ireland—*every* place was our home. But, funny enough, I was born in Dublin, in the old Coombe Hospital, when there was a big snowstorm. I remember me father telling me about the big fall of snow, and he'd all his horses and caravan out and we took a tenement room in High Street. There was *always* a distinction about our life: we were the *travelling people*, and we wasn't wanted in many spots in the country. If you started to put a fire on the ground the police would come and might kick it up in your face. Ah, the police were very hard on us years ago. Not because we'd be robbing or doing anything, but just because we were the travelling people."

(Margaret Doran Murphy, traveller)

"Lugs Branigan, he got his reputation around the Liberties from fighting, going in and out of the likes of the tinkers. There used to be a couple of old yards there and there was about ten caravans there. If there was a row with them he'd go in and he'd fight the best of them. And they were hard men, them fellas. They could fight. And it was all bare knuckle. Most of them were chimney sweeps. We used to love to see them fight—and the women were better than the men! They'd make a ring for the women to box. No hair-pulling, actually boxing!"

(John Joe Kennedy, age 75)

"Unfortunately, the early history of Ireland's travelling people is obscure. Being illiterate, they left no written records of their own. Being poor, they largely have been ignored in the literature of the 'Great Tradition'."

(Sharon Gmelch, anthropologist)

"It appears that Tinkers value survival by one's wits, the inner wisdom that comes from cruel experiences of the life on the road and respect for the family more highly than the possession of a set of educationally derived conventions existing outside their cultural context."

(Martina Ó Fearadhaigh)

"Dublin would be a dull place without her crowd of little ones, high and low, and, if the noise of them playing in the streets is sometimes disturbing, think of the alternative. And as the little noses are pressed against the windows of the toy shops and the confectioners', remember that youth is fleeting, and take pleasure in the gladness and joy of childhood that surrounds us while it lasts."

(A. Peter)

"Folksy nostalgia has created the illusion that somehow the real Dublin is dead. Rather than being dead it is alive and vibrant with new people, with new blood, new streets, new place names. Its history is not finished but yet to be written by the masses of children who are still living it."

(Dermot Bolger)

Chris Carr

"To understand the city one has to understand the neighbourhoods that make it up."

(Gerry Cahill)

"I was told about the artisans' dwellings and I got to know everybody up there. And they were the *loveliest* people. Those people up around Oxmantown Road and Ivar Street are special people, the salt of the earth as far as I was concerned. It's a real little close-knit community. This was my neighbourhood. People knew me as a fair cop. I always treated them as humans, and they respected me for that."

(John Barry, garda)

"People in the artisans' dwellings, they've always been great neighbours. People who cared about others. Nobody had very much, but everybody shared. I can remember the night my father died and neighbours coming in with two or three eggs for my mother and a half a loaf of bread and a bottle of milk. After my father died my mother had to go to work, and I was reared by neighbours."

(Éamonn O'Brien)

"There's nothing very glamorous about the Buildings. They are what they are—artisans' dwellings. And they're stereotyped. Buildings that of themselves are not much to look at. But as a *pattern* they have a certain *style* that is worth preserving. There's an aura, a feeling, about it that is worthy of preservation."

(Thomas Linehan)

"I was born up on Malachi Road. It was a good area to grow up in. There were forty-one houses on the road, and everyone knew everyone else. If the door wasn't open by half-nine in the morning somebody would go over to find out what was wrong. Everybody knew what everybody else had, and everybody shared. My favourite story is the Christmas pudding cloth. There was only one in the street. It was a square of calico, and a Mrs Murphy had that. She had a little notebook to go with it. And it would go around—so everybody had to decide when they were going to make their Christmas pudding."

(Tony Morris)

Éamonn Crowe, stone-carver

"My father taught me everything: lettering, carving, interlacing crosses, figurework, foliage. Stone-carvers lived for their work. It was obsessive. It was pride in what they were doing. Our carving is still all done by hand, but a lot of them now are using machines, because they can't use their hands. We're a dying breed. It's inevitable."

(Éamonn Crowe, stone-carver)

Leslie Foy,
signwriter

"A signwriter is artistic, he can do all styles of lettering—old English, roman, gothic. Lettering should have an artistic flow about it. Some is very elaborate three-dimensional work, with highlights and shadows. People stop and watch you working on a job, standing around at the bottom of the plank. I think it's a compliment. And maybe sometimes I'll play to the gallery. Dublin people are great critics, and they'll come out of a pub and give their expert critique."

(Leslie Foy, signwriter)

"If you are lucky enough to be born into a comfortable middle-class home then you have a future, you go to college, you choose a career. If you are born into an inner-city flats complex, then you struggle to survive."

(Tony Gregory)

"From the age of two I was reared 'on the street.' The street was where it all, or most of it, happened for me. I could play from early morning, when I rushed out into the street clean and shiny, until late at night when I was dragged into the house filthy dirty and sometimes black and blue from whatever the situations of play might have thrown up."

(Patrick Boland)

"Many inner-city areas have high-rise flats, where children are trapped. They seldom see anything to express their humanity like trees and greenery."

(Father Paul Lavelle)

"In 1958, after I left Castleknock College at eighteen years of age, I was shocked to discover another world in Dublin city in such places as Benburb Street, Seán MacDermott Street. It was one of deprivation, little opportunity for education and very real poverty. I have tried to introduce boys and girls from a background similar to mine to that world. Each side does not know how the other side lives! These eighteen-year-olds live for forty-eight hours in deprived areas of Dublin. The Urban Plunge sets out to build a bridge between cultures. One of the main learning experiences for 'plungers' is the sense of community that does not appear to be present in the more affluent areas ... the inner city is rich in human qualities such as neighbourliness, compassion, resilience and a good sense of humour. Unless the wealthy elements in society have an understanding of the (inner-city) problems there is very little chance of their responding to the situation. The Urban Plunge makes the better off, better educated more aware of these problems ... it builds bridges between groups of people from very different backgrounds."

(Father Paul Lavelle)

"Lined old faces appear at decaying windows to look down on streets littered with blown paper scraps, on sons and daughters as they sit on doorsteps against a background of graffiti, while the grandchildren crawl or sprawl on the dirty pavements."

(Brendan Lehane)

"My first experience at busking was here in Dublin up in Grafton Street. I walked up Grafton Street and took out my guitar and started playing. My knees were like jelly ... shaking. And I put it back in the box and walked up the street. Then I said to myself, '*I have to do it!* It was desperation, I was broke. So I walked back down again, and three or four months later I was an old busker."

(Frank Quinlan)

"Grafton Street is the morning promenade for the well-to-do fashionable members of both sexes. Exhibitionists of the latest models in women's, and men's wear, amble slowly along through the crowds. After a half an hour's sauntering, these 'fashion-plates' waft into the stylish cafés for a cup of morning coffee, and there they get down to the serious business of analysing and criticising each other. Dubliners of the solid type get quite a bit of fun out of the morning walk in Grafton Street, because neither fashions nor freaks are taken seriously."

(G. Ivan Morris)

"When I set about gathering my thoughts on Dublin over seventy years ago, I found it difficult to realise that I am still living in the same city among the same people. Comparing Dublin then with today would make a Cinderella-like fairy tale. The pinch-faced, ragged, bare-footed children running along the cobble-stoned streets have been replaced by trendily dressed, well-shod youths."

(Moira Lysaght)

Smithfield

Smithfield

"From the time I was knee-high I remember nothing else but going around buying horses, selling horses. It was just in the blood. I was *born* with horses. Horses and cattle and pigs flying about the streets, it was a familiar sight in Dublin, just a part of the street life."

(Antoinette Cooper Healy, horse-dealer)

Smithfield

"I never missed the horse fair in Smithfield. All the horse-dealers would go to Smithfield to a very old pub, Peter Donoghue's, and talk horses, make deals, have a drink, and have a good bit of chat. My father and grandfather was in the horse-dealing. Oh, I'd be the fourth generation in it. I'd be dressed clearly as a dealer, always a nice blue suit and shoes and a hat. I done business fair and honest, and horse-dealers always carried only cash. And the slapping and spitting in your hand when you'd buy a horse, that was a great tradition."

(John Mannion, horse-dealer)

Brian Hudson, pavement artist

College Green

"We're called 'chalkies' in Dublin. I put colour and an image on just a grey ground and that's a contribution. Dubliners appreciate it. I'd be out for about six hours and I might take out two hundred pieces of chalk. The lovely thing is that there isn't a brush between you and your picture. It's your fingers. But blending the chalks with my fingers I'm rubbing the skin away. And on pavement it's your knees that hurt the most. It's the motivation to *create* something, a way of expression. People come up and say, 'You're a very talented artist.' A thousand people might see it—and then it's *gone.*"

(Brian Hudson, pavement artist)

Ursula Meehan, pavement artist

"You have to be a free spirit. I've always felt it was worth people giving money for street drawing, because you'd made something beautiful. I love seeing the colour you're doing on the street. That attracts people, and for the moment people enjoy it."

(Ursula Meehan, pavement artist)

College Green

Cumberland Street

There's No Time Like Guinness Time

"All our clothes came from Cumberland Street, that was the 'Hill'. Local people'd sell the old clothes, they'd get them from the tuggers going around and knocking on doors. We only lived around the corner and I'd go with my mother and she'd just root out old trousers and stockings."

(Jimmy McLoughlin)

Cumberland Street

"The clothing, they were second-hand. But some good clothes, perfectly clean. See, the tuggers'd go from house to house, very well-off ladies' houses, and buy what the wife had. People weren't ashamed at that time, they'd try it on over their frock. They were second-hand, but you'd be dressed up for a funeral!"

(Annie Ryan, market dealer)

Cumberland Street

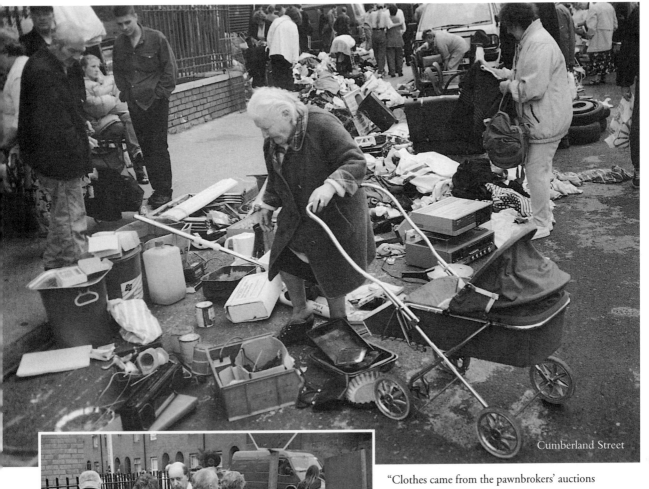

Cumberland Street

"Clothes came from the pawnbrokers' auctions and jumble sales. Protestant halls would always hold a jumble sale, some Catholic halls too. We'd go with me mother, bring around the cart and wheel it for her. There'd be *everything*: clothes and shoes and handbags, hats, hardware. Oh, we'd all go mad to root through them. It was grand."

(Kathleen Maguire, market dealer)

The Gypsy Lee

"As kids we could stand on the wall and see all the weddings, 'cause our tenement was next to the church. The girl and fella got married and come out of Francis Street chapel, and you'd see them out skipping rope on the street. Married but skipping rope! They were innocent. And the groom would throw out a few coppers in a brown bag to the kids. Ha'pennies and pennies. Oh, yeah, that was called the 'grushie'."

(Mary Doolan, age 78)

Sarah Murray

"You'd want to hear the old people talking to realise the *faith* they have, the love for the church and the priest. Unquestioned faith. They were born with it. It's hard to define, but it's there. You can *sense* it. It's a faith with which they accepted everything they were told by the church. If the priest says it, it must be right. That type of faith will die out."

(Father Brendan Lawless)

Kathleen Maguire

"At that time the girls and boys growing up was really innocent. Oh, definitely ... their little ways of skipping and everything. All we ever done to get a fella when we were young was rob their caps. If you fancied a fella you robbed his cap and you ran, and he ran after you."

(May Hanaphy, age 92)

Maisie Daly

"I'm not telling a lie now, my mother was a saint, a *living* saint. My poor mother done her washing with her board and used to kneel down with a bucket and water and have things like *milk*. She never drank and never smoked. And *never* had a holiday. But she used to go to the Moira Hall, the Mothers' Club, and they got a cup of tea and a biscuit, and said the Rosary. And she lived for that every Tuesday."

(Mary Doolan, age 78)

"When you were courting you'd stand for hours talking and chatting, and there wasn't a bit of harm. And we always went window-shopping in Grafton Street and O'Connell Street. And you didn't hold hands then, you linked arms. Morals were very high. When I think how harmless we were … pure innocence at seventeen and eighteen."

(Mary Bolton, age 81)

Mary Casey

Anastasia Barry

"We had a very happy life. The weekend was kind of a family get-together, and we always had cards. And we had a gramophone and we'd play a lot of records, John McCormack at that stage. And we had a piano and two of my sisters played on a Sunday. And conversation! Oh, Lord, people listened to each other!"

(Winifred Keogh, age 70)

"It's an old-fashioned kind of shop. I dress the windows every morning, mostly sausages, bacon, ham, cereals, and jams and fruit. It looks real good. We still hang the bacon and hams on those bars. Very few shops do it now. Even people coming back from England will bring their kids in and show them."

(Joseph Moore, butcher and small grocer)

"I bought this shop in 1945, it must be two hundred years old. We used to live above the shop. Sure, I knew everyone in the neighbourhood. We'd sell pigs' crubeens, cabbages and eggs and cigarettes loose. And weigh up our sugar and tea and spices, mostly nutmeg and cloves. And we used to dress the window in them years. Oh, God, yes, you had to dress the window: that was a kind of trade in them days. You'd put *everything* in the window. And at Christmas a lot of cakes and hams."

(William Walshe, small grocer)

Smithfield

"When the cry was raised 'Runaway horse!' there was a scatter in all directions. Children were grabbed by parents and hustled into homes or shops or doorways. One afternoon I witnessed a brave act. I was standing at the corner of Red Cow Lane in Smithfield. A runaway horse came careering along King Street towards Smithfield. A DMP man, hearing the commotion, took off his cape and, running with the horse, he very expertly threw the cape over the animal's head. The horse stopped dead."

(Paddy Crosbie)

"A runaway horse was as good as a cowboy film. It was hair-raising to watch the driver bent backwards like a rodeo rider straining and pulling on the reins, yelling 'Hike, ho-there, ho-there,' at the top of his voice, as the animal bolted. In winter time when the roads were covered with ice and frost the horses provided us with more drama. They slipped and skidded all over the roads and cobblestones."

(Máirín Johnston)

"Of Dublin's many distinctions, possibly the most nearly unique is that of impromptu conversation, the most spontaneous and evanescent of the arts."

(Richard M. Kain)

"Human scale has been preserved here, so that the individual personality is complemented rather than dwarfed by the architecture, allowing the city to retain a distinctive atmosphere conducive to gossipaceous creativity."

(David Norris)

"In a little city like Dublin one meets every person whom one knows within a few days. Around each bend in the road there is a friend, an enemy, or a bore striding towards you, so that, with a piety which is almost religious, one says 'touch wood' before turning any corner."

(James Stephens)

"Talk was entertainment, and there was plenty of it. Television, the great conversation-killer of today, wasn't heard of, and even the humble wireless was a bit of a novelty. I was eighteen before my mother allowed one into the [tenement] room. She thought they were a terrible waste of money, because you could get enough news and entertainment talking to your neighbours ... There was no shortage of opportunity to indulge in 'oul chat'."

(Máirín Johnston)

O'Connell Bridge

O'Connell Bridge

"The begging strategy of traveller women in Dublin is to evoke sympathy and compassion. Tinkers work to create the impression that they are destitute. She wears old clothing, often soiled and tattered, also the traditional shawl or 'rug'. The presence of a child or infant is an important element in begging strategy. Travellers are aware of the sympathy for their children."

(George Gmelch)

"I used to watch beggars from the top window of a Dublin restaurant. Young pretty girls and young men accompanying women were generous, but most people avoided beggars as if they had the plague. And indeed they have—the plague of misfortune. A husband that drinks; a family of ten; illness ... causes that reduce a Dublin woman to begging."

(Olivia Robertson)

Grafton Street

"Of all the ballad-singers who came around Pimlico, none could compare with John Wilson. Around his shoulders he wore an old leather cloak which fastened under his chin and was open down the front. His accordion was strapped under this from his shoulders and on his head he wore a battered slouched hat which gave him a very rakish appearance. All the windows in the tenements would go up, heads and half bodies would lean out, while the ha'pennies, thrupenny bits and sometimes even sixpences were tossed down from the windows."

(Máirín Johnston)

Grafton Street

"If itinerant hawkers were plentiful a hundred years ago, so too were itinerant musicians; the artists of the piercing tin whistle, and the fiddlers—often blind, alas! But it was the ballad singers who drew the crowds. Their songs were usually topical and witty."

(Brian Mac Giolla Phádraig)

"Characters there were in plenty ... the streets of Dublin then were thronged with them. A lady in a shawl played the banjo and did a step dance outside Bill Bushe's pub a couple of times a week. She knew only one tune, 'Mick McGilligan's Daughter, Mary-Anne', which was the only name by which she was identified."

(Bill Kelly)

Smithfield

"We'd no playgrounds in those days and I lived next to a forge. Great memories of that. The farrier, he was a very big man, very broad. We'd stand there and smell the forge when he'd be burning the hoof. Lovely smells would come out of it."

(Jimmy McLoughlin)

"The smith is celebrated in song and story. In ancient times the smith was a man of high social standing. He came next after the professional class, the judges, poets, physicians and clergy, and often dined at the table of the high king. But, like everything else, the smith's job is changing ... a lessening number of horses to be shod. You could hear the tones of regret in the smith's voice, the regret of the hereditary craftsman whose real skill and talent were so seldom required today."

(Kevin Danaher)

Simple scrawlings
Silent statements,
Blare the plight
Of people's lives.

Declarations
Proclamations,
Words of warning
"We'll survive!"
                              (KCK)

"Poverty need not preclude learning to draw and paint, or playing the violin, having fun, or loving and being loved."
                              (Francis Stuart)

"The people themselves would band together and confront the pushers and demand that they would either stop pushing or leave the area. The effort was made by some of the poorest and most powerless in society. The people discovered their own power through renewing the sense of community."

(Ronan Sheehan and Brendan Walsh)

"City centre communities have fought tenaciously to regain control over their lives ... drug pushers are being driven out ... the city centre is fighting back."

(Peter Sheridan)

There was eviction—I seen it hundreds of times. They couldn't pay their rent. They'd throw you out into the street in the snow and everything. And at that time the Corporation didn't care. That was the way it was. Loads of people put out. And maybe they'd reared a family there. Throw bed clothes and all out into the street ... and them poor people sitting out there in the street in the chairs."

(Timmy Kirwan)

"The area is full of small acts of heroism. The heroin problem in the north inner city is beaten by the people. It was the mothers and fathers who said they had had enough, who marched under threats of intimidation and violence, to the pushers' houses and said 'Out, out, out!'"

(Mick Rafferty)

Jim Cruite, saddler

"It was completely different years ago. People bringing in their stuff all the time. Firms like dairies had sixty or seventy horses. I like people coming in to talk to me today, they love the smell of leather. Little children love to come in and see the old harnesses and saddles, the old things their grandfathers used to have ... but I miss the horses trotting by."

(John Cruite, saddler)

Sam Greer, saddler

Jim Cruite, saddler

"During the war years my father had five men working in here. Plenty of work at that time. They used to bring the horses right up here to the shop. Today it's amazing the number of people going by the door saying, 'I didn't think there were any saddlers left in the city.' It must be the most photographed shop in Ireland."

(Sam Greer, saddler)

Liam Preston, spieler

"I'm a spieler. We 'spiel' them. Spieling means to get out and actually do it differently than just standing there selling ... to give a good speech, a good line of speech. If we just put out gold chains on a board people'd just walk by us. Make 'em think it's too good to be true: three gold chains for only three pounds! You've got to get them to stop first—then hold them. Curiosity! They'll stop. It's a stage there. You'll get good pitches and it'd be a great crowd, and you'd get really good laughs. Ah, I see meself as a performer. I have jokes and all. Before I even talk about jewellery I give them a few laughs, because it brightens up their day."

(Liam Preston, Henry Street spieler)

Pintman Paddy Losty

"Dooley's, that was one of the most famous pubs around when I started drinking, about 1935. Now there was plenty of other pints along the quay, but *that* pint, I'll tell you, it was always perfect. Oh, what a drink! They had one of the best cellars in Dublin. Pulled from the barrel down below, and you could *feel* the substance of it. And *no rush*. It might take ten minutes to bring it to a head, the cream. Oh, lovely. You could drink about twenty of them and the next morning you'd be like a two-year-old, there'd be no hangover. Yes, sir."

(Tommy Murray, true pintman)

"The true pintman always approaches his pint with reverence in a contemplative fashion, and a tranquil state of mind. He does not even need to be in company, for his pint is his company. If you study the good pintman in a pub you will observe how he can stand staring into the glass for long periods, thinking deep thoughts. This is because he knows that truth lies at the bottom of the glass."

(Tom Corkery)

Pintman Luke Nugent

"When things go wrong and will not come right,
Though you do the best you can,
When life looks black as the hours of night—
A pint of plain is your only man."

(Flann O'Brien)

"Yes! ... he's a child of the inner city
And the fact that he knows is more the pity
Drinking cider since he was seven
Old as the hills and he's only eleven."

(Pete St John)

"Away from the main thoroughfares, Dublin seems to be a city of children. The combination of large families and cramped housing conspired to make the grey back streets a teeming playground, where toddlers take their first steps, older boys and girls gather in impromptu gangs—and adults rarely seem to intrude."

(Brendan Lehane)

"Bugsy Malone Gang" (1976)

"Years ago when there was a row there was no wooden bars or chains. And all the fellas was very handy, they could use their hands! No need for weapons. They were great, all in boxing clubs. They were called 'bread and tea' boxers because they had no food. It was hand-to-hand and they'd shake hands when they'd finished. Oh, but gang warfare was a different thing. Oh, yes! Ten or twelve fighting. And then they'd use weapons. I seen that all the time."

(Timmy Kirwan)

"We lived on Pimlico and for devilment we always picked on old people, I don't know why. It's the demon in kids. But if they caught you, you could get a licking! There were all different gangs and cliques of kids and you'd see a group hovering around and you didn't do down to them because they were the tough guys. They were down on Ash Street and the Coombe. If they seen me with money, going for messages, they'd stop me and take the money off me. Your parents would be docile and say, 'Oh, forget about it!', 'cause they didn't want to become involved."

(Stephen Mooney)

"Our fashionable shopping areas are in between Kildare Street and Grafton Street. Switzer's is the very home of Anglo-Irish clothes—one sees felt sporting hats in the windows. Brown Thomas rules the other side of Grafton Street and suggests the new culture. There you see hats with flowers and veils. As a child, I almost understood the difference between Catholics and Protestants by looking at Switzer's and Brown Thomas hats."

(Olivia Robertson)

Greene's Bookshop, Clare Street

"Now there were two stands out there, and then my father put that canopy up about 1917. And he got an extra four stands, and we had *six* stands then, with books ranging from a penny up to a shilling, and people'd come and browse through the second-hand books. It was a browser's paradise! It was a different clientele then. I mean, we had W. B. Yeats and George Russell and Jack B. Yeats, and Samuel Beckett often came in. Greene's is an institution!"

(Herbert Pembrey, proprietor of Greene's Bookshop)

Dublin's Fruit and Vegetable Markets

"Horses do not fear the machine, they despise it and retard it. Have you never experienced, in a narrow Dublin street, the glorious sight and sounds of a long line of frustrated juggernauts, howling and honking and bleating with rage behind the calm indifferent progress of some stately shire or tough Irish draught? I regret the passing of the horse from so many of his functions, from the bread van and from the post office. And I know that I would prefer to be nearly killed any day by a horseman than by a motorman."

(Tom Corkery)

"The last firm in Dublin to keep horses was Dublin Dairies. They went down from about twenty to only four or five. They kept cutting down. They went into the sixties, they were the last. In a couple of years you'll hear children say, 'Oh, there's a horse, Mammy!' And that day is coming very fast."

(Pat Cooper, horse-dealer)

"Dublin was all horses then. Five hundred horses lining up in O'Connell Street in the morning. *Unbelievable.* Oh, yes, jarveys, CIE, bakeries. In the *heart* of Dublin. Everywhere you looked there were horses. The great ruination of Ireland was to take the horse off the street. Oh, the horse age in Dublin is dying out ... but there's still plenty of horsemen around Dublin."

(John Mannion, horse-dealer)

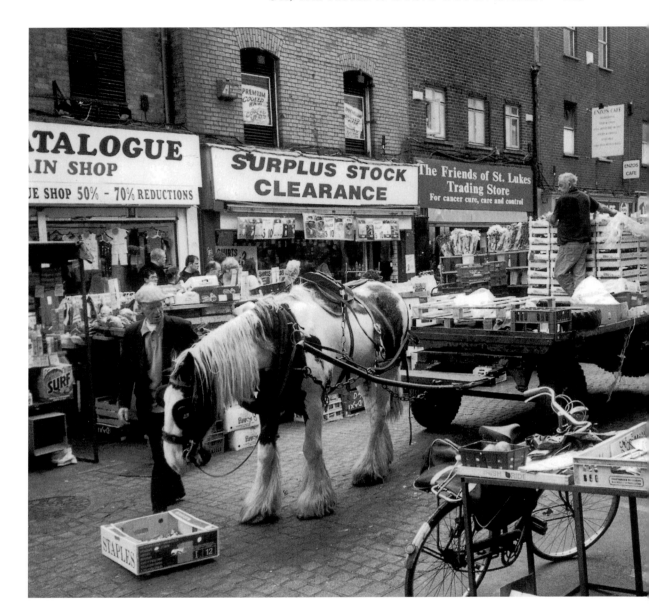

"There were horses everywhere; on every street corner there was a horse coming around it. You can never bring the grace of a horse to a car. I still jump up to the window when I hear the cloppety-clop sound of a horse going by. Horses nearly went off the road altogether, but the nostalgia won't die."

(Antoinette Cooper Healy, horse-dealer)

"The label 'inner city', more specifically the 'north inner city'—the phrase is not of Dublin coinage, and even now you will rarely hear older people use it. It suggests a category rather than a place, a malaise rather than a situation. It cheats the citizen of his or her identity. The powerful label the powerless."

(Ronan Sheehan and Brendan Walsh)

"The north inner city has been and is the most publicised of Dublin's districts—for all the wrong reasons ... unemployment, lawlessness, drug addiction and despair ... [but] other aspects of the area are hospitality, its hope, its neighbourliness, its culture."

(Father Peter Lemass and Father Paul Lavelle)

"When the population of the city was comfortably below half a million, city dwellers identified with the street, the neighbourhood, the parish; 'inner city' would have been an inconceivable term to natives of Waterford Street, the Monto, the Diamond, Summerhill, Corporation Street and various other small units which prevailed."

(Ronan Sheehan)

Pigeon lofts behind Iveagh Buildings

"Pigeon-racing has been a great part of the history of Dublin. In the poor tenement areas the pigeon-fancier, that was his sole hobby ... that was his *religion*! And he would deny himself his pint or his cigarettes to save up and buy something for his pigeon loft."

(Tony Kiely)

"Oh, the women were very proud of their washing, and it was always lovely and clean. They'd have a line stick, a pole, shoved out through the window to hang their washing on. And very critical of one another in them years. If they put out anything that wasn't washed well they'd say, 'Oooh, look at her wash!'"

(Nancy Cullen)

"North Dublin, to the strict aesthete, is a disgrace. Like classic Irish greatcoats—bulky drapes of Donegal tweed that comprehensively protect against the weather—it serves a useful purpose for people with more important things than appearance to think, talk, worry, fight and sing about. It fits badly and hangs loosely; but its inhabitants seem neither to notice nor care. Their words flow, their consciousnesses stream, without regard to their physical setting."

(Brendan Lehane)

Smithfield

"The children ... with indeflectable purpose break open the water mains ... until high and glorious fountains rise into the light ... They run back and forward beneath the spray like holy dervishes."

(Pádraig J. Daly)

"No matter what conventional playgrounds are provided for children to keep them off the streets they will always prefer the thrills and excitement of swinging on a lamp-post and performing all sorts of acrobatic feats."

(Éilís Brady)

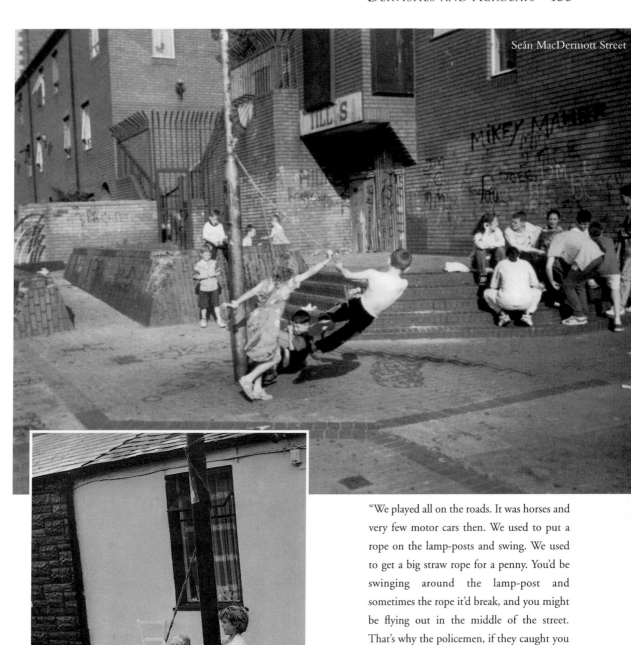

Seán MacDermott Street

"We played all on the roads. It was horses and very few motor cars then. We used to put a rope on the lamp-posts and swing. We used to get a big straw rope for a penny. You'd be swinging around the lamp-post and sometimes the rope it'd break, and you might be flying out in the middle of the street. That's why the policemen, if they caught you swinging on a lamp-post, they'd cut your rope and you'd have to run."

(Mary Waldron)

"Down in the Alley-O,
Where we play Relieve-e-O,
Up comes her mother-O,
Have you seen me Katie-O?
She's down in the Alley-O,
Kissing all the Fellas-O."

(Old Dublin song)

"On the west side of Smithfield there is a passageway which bears the mystifying name of Thundercut Alley. This derives from a brewery—Thunder's—in the early eighteenth century. Workers in the brewery from the Stoneybatter area used to take a short-cut to Smithfield; the short-cut came to be known as Thunder Cut. When houses were built the right of way remained to become an alley-way."

(Paddy Crosbie)

"The children themselves are uniquely of Ireland—and Dublin. They wear clothes as brilliantly coloured as the Book of Kells and their hair ... flaxen, nut-brown, gold, and above all red— vermillion, orange-red, ginger and copper, hair the 'red-gold' of legend ... it is always with us, brightening a group of children in Gardiner or Hill Street with cheerful warmth as they skip in the sun."

(Olivia Robertson)

"The sweetest roamer is a boy's young heart"
(George Edward Woodberry)

"I have had playmates,
I have had companions,
In my days of childhood,
In my joyful school days —
All, all are gone,
The old familiar faces."
(Charles Lamb)

Iveagh Market

"When me father brings his wages home,
At tea-time, Friday night,
I run out and get the milk
An' the table-cloth's snow white.
Me mother gives him two boiled eggs,
An' the fire is grand and bright,
When me father brings his wages home,
At tea-time, Friday night."

(Anonymous)

"The metal casks really began to appear in the fifties. Coopers didn't like them, they called them 'depth charges' and 'iron lungs'. Coopers saw them as a threat to the old craft—saw their world changing. They were going into Guinness's and there was no way to stop them. Things were becoming increasingly slack, and the men knew that some would have to be let go."

(Eddie Dunne, cooper)

One of the most artistic, albeit often missed, relics of early Georgian "street furniture" are the cast-iron coal-hole covers implanted along the pavements. The coal-holes were delivery chutes to expansive cellars below ground. Most have been badly eroded by infinite pedestrian tramplings since their casting date (*c.* 1760–1830). However, some still retain fine detail and dimension and are very pleasing to the discerning eye.

"Dublin possesses one of the most unique collections of street furniture in Europe."
(Derry O'Connell)

"Street games began to absorb the long afternoons until meal time came on, and the gas lamps one after the other were lit up. Handball was played against a high gable wall, with scouts to cry 'Nix' or 'Harvey Duff' if any bobby came in sight, for the DMP discouraged ball games."

(C. P. Curran)

"When we were young we were 'youngsters' or 'chislers'—never teenagers. In those days we acquired more education on the streets than in school."

(Máirín Johnston)

"I envy children, they are the only true explorers. To their anticipatory eyes every street corner is an adventure, every garden wall a challenge. We snap at them when out walking because they must be up every blind alley and down every hole in the road. And we forget the buoyant days of our own childhood, when every hole in the wall was an opening to goblin-land, every curtained window a screen for cabalistic goings-on."

(Tom Corkery)

Moore Street

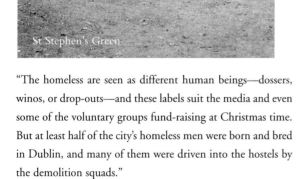

St Stephen's Green

"The elderly, living alone, are often the forgotten people of our society."

(Dónal Storey)

"The homeless are seen as different human beings—dossers, winos, or drop-outs—and these labels suit the media and even some of the voluntary groups fund-raising at Christmas time. But at least half of the city's homeless men were born and bred in Dublin, and many of them were driven into the hostels by the demolition squads."

(Alice Leahy)

Dermot Broe, stone-carver

"There was more pipe-smoking years ago, and it was more of an art than it is today ... but there are still people who regard pipe-smoking as an art. People can give up cigarettes, but when they give up a pipe they feel they've lost a *friend*. People who smoke pipes always seem to be relaxed. There's a great aura about them, that they're capable of dealing with situations. Even an old man, although he mightn't be able to get around much, if he's able to sit and you see him smoking his pipe, there's a *friend* with him!"

(David McGrane, tobacconist and cigar merchant)

"I have seen a man stop a tram in College Green, strike a
match on it, light his pipe, and nod his thanks to the driver.
And the driver only grinned and cursed him in a friendly way."
(P. L. Dickinson)

"After a baby's birth, the Jubilee Nurse would come around daily to attend to the mother and child. She was a very familiar figure around our street in those days (1930s). Sometimes she arrived on a bike and we would all rush over to her to ask if we could mind it for her. These nurses were so kind that they were known around our way as 'angels of mercy'."

(Máirín Johnston)

Glue-sniffers, O'Connell Street

"Today's kids ... they sniff their glue, get stoned on drugs ... the old fogies wag their heads wisely, gravely tut-tut and wonder what is wrong with the young people of today. What indeed! ... some inheritance we have given them."

(Lar Redmond)

"Of all the pleasures that alcohol lubricates, none is as widespread in Dublin as that team of temptresses, horses and the gambling they give rise to. When a dozen or so yearlings or fillies line up under their midget riders, men and women are placing their last wagers in the crowded betting shops ... to bet a pound, two, five, any denomination up to a thousand or more, in a continuous redistribution of the national income. Then it's briskly over. A few people, suppressing their elation, collect their winnings with shifty looks. The rest hope for better luck next time ... and many swear this time will be the last."

(Brendan Lehane)

"Betting is a subject that is seldom far from the tongue of an Irishman. The Irish are a sporting people who, whether they win, lose or draw, still get an immense satisfaction out of the excitement of having money on the horse of their fancy—a horse, perhaps, whose form they have studied since his birth, whose very tail-hairs they have numbered."

(G. Ivan Morris)

Tugger in Meath Street

"Every day I pushed me pram on the road in the traffic. *Every day*. There was horses and cars, and we'd be walking through them. Keep walking. And we had to push the prams over the cobblestones, and it was really very hard, it was. If you were bringing down [heavy] bananas or oranges the pram wouldn't last two months. I got a pram back then used for maybe two, three shillings. I must have had sixty prams in my lifetime."

(Ellen Preston, street dealer)

Arbour Hill

"Part of the charm of Dublin is the rural quality seen in pockets all over the city."

(Deirdre Kelly)

Muareen Lynch's cottage, Royal Canal and North Strand

"This cottage would be over two hundred years old. Seven of us reared here, and not one ever fell into the canal. Ah, it was lovely here. We used to have cabbage and rhubarb and potatoes on the canal banks. We had a pony, Molly, and a nannygoat. And there were swans and geese in the canal. And it was nice when you'd see the horses that belonged to the bargemen. And make their tea out of water from the canal, it was *that clean*."

(Maureen Lynch, cottage-dweller)

Harry Barnwell, shoemaker, in shop in Castle Street

"In my time a lot of boys in St Werburgh's parish were shoemakers. Around the Liberties they would take a boy on for a seven-year indenture. By the time I was nineteen you couldn't teach me any more about it. When my apprenticeship started I was paid half a crown. Times were hard, make no mistake about it. There was no electric, so you had a candle on your stool. You'd be sitting there for five straight hours. Some days I used to work here in the shop until one in the morning. Your hands would be sore, because you were boring all day through tough leather. Physically hard work. But there's more to a job than money, you know. You must have love. Soon this little shop will be closed and I'll be up in Heaven with me little hammer, making shoes for the angels."

(Harry Barnwell, last shoemaker in the Liberties)

Lauri Grennell, Parnell Street

"There were dozens of shoemakers in Dublin in the thirties, and competition was great. It's physically hard work. And shoemakers were always badly paid. I often pawned my watch to get money for leather in the bad old days. I'm not a bit ashamed to say that. I used to work long hours, sometimes to eleven when I was rearing a family. Tailors and shoemakers were always a clan, and recognised as great drinkers. I suppose it was an outlet for their frustrations, for their worries and troubles. Shoemakers will disappear completely. We're definitely the last—the end of the clan."

(Tommy Malone, shoemaker)

John Ryan, Grattan Street

"The best way to lengthen out our days is to walk steadily and with a purpose."

(Charles Dickens)

I go back four generations, to me great-grandfather, in pigs. Helping me father out in the yard since I was five. There's not many pig-raisers around now. Raising pigs now in the city is outdated, like keeping chickens and hens. But I spent me life in it. I'm just seeing an old thing out, you know?"

(Jimmy Riley)

Jimmy Riley, North King Street

Billy Storey, pig-raiser, Manor Street Mews

"From me grandfather, pigs were part and parcel of the family. It's in the blood. I've been in this lane for thirty-eight years now. Normally we kept about forty pigs here. I have only seven now. Very few places in the world now where you'd get pigs in the city. People come down the lane and they can't believe there's still pigs here. It keeps a few bob together. But the Corporation can come down any day now and take away the lane. The writing is on the wall for that."

(Paddy Doyle, pig-raiser)

Paddy Doyle, pig-raiser, Oxmantown Lane

"In the summertime everybody would be sitting out. They'd bring their chairs out, and there'd be another group on the other side of the street. Women would chat, be sewing, knitting. The men would sit and play cards and play handball at the top of the street. We all left babies out in the prams at the windows. If it was a warm night we'd be sitting out late talking, until twelve or one."

(Bridget McDonagh)

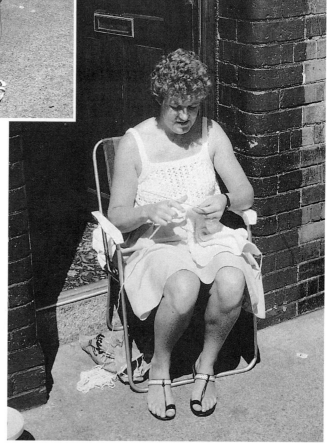

"Haymarket days held in Smithfield created a hum of industry, the horse-drawn carts top heavy with hay adding their fragrance to the picturesque scene. Grainwash from the nearby Jameson's Distillery was shovelled from big vat-like lorries into farmers' carts for animal feeding. Farmers strode along with their whips tied in bandolier fashion over their shoulders, and unpretentious restaurants and sleeping accommodations were to be found to facilitate visiting farmers and dealers. And there were coach builders, harness makers, and farriers, many with living quarters above their premises. Tinkers dealt in horses, asses and mules. On those market days the usual occupational sounds were occasionally drowned by the braying of a tinker's ass, but much more blood-curdling was the cry of some of its owners with all the troupe joining in and blood being spilt and hair flying in the faction fighting fashion of olden days."

(Moira Lysaght)

"Daddy Egan, who owned a pub at the north end of Smithfield, was a grey-haired old man who stopped children on the street to give each a prayer leaflet plus a penny to light a candle. I am afraid that most of us spent the money on sweets."

(Paddy Crosbie)

Moore Street

"My father started selling papers, and I was down on the corner with him since I was eight years old. The *Herald* and the *Mail* were the biggest back then; they were a penny-ha'pence. I don't mind the cold or rain. I feel like it's home on the corner here. A lady brings me over a flask of tea every day and she stays with me and we have a little chat. It's alive. I'm never bored."

(Dina Moore, paper-seller)

Dina Moore, left

"They all know me as the paper-man on Hanlon's Corner. I'm here in the morning at a quarter past seven. People like to have a bit of chat, and I know nearly all that goes on. But there are some people you can't talk to, story-carriers looking to find if you knew anything so they could talk about it. You keep your mouth shut, you know? Just play stupid."

(Billy Arthurs, paper-seller)

Billy Arthurs

"A colourful street is Moore Street, where the street traders sell fruit, flowers and vegetables at low prices to the accompaniment of back-chat, wisecracks and many a verbal battle. The symphonic smell of Moore Street, so many smells in one, is unique; no other street in Dublin has a smell like it, and this, coupled with the litter of orange peel, cabbage leaves, and other refuse, marks the place in the memory of the visitor as the 'cornucopia' of Dublin."

(G. Ivan Morri)

"In Dublin's fair city, where the girls are so pretty,
I first set my eyes on sweet Molly Malone,
As she wheeled her wheelbarrow through streets broad and narrow,
Crying, 'Cockles! And mussels! Alive, alive-o!'"

Moore Street

"Time drops in decay,
Like a candle burnt out."
(W. B. Yeats)

SUGGESTED READINGS

Chart, D. A., *The Story of Dublin,* London: J. M. Dent 1932.

Clarke, Desmond, *Dublin,* London: B. T. Batsford 1977

Collins, James, *Life in Old Dublin,* Cork: Tower Books 1978 (reprint of original edition 1913).

Corkery, Tom, *Tom Corkery's Dublin,* Dublin: Anvil Press 1980.

Crosbie, Paddy, *Your Dinner's Poured Out!,* Dublin: O'Brien Press 1981.

Crowley, Elaine, *Cowslips and Chainies: A Memoir of Dublin in the 1930s,* Dublin: Lilliput Press 1996.

Daly, Mary E., *Dublin: The Deposed Capital,* Cork: Cork University Press 1984.

Davies, Sidney, *Dublin Types,* Dublin: Talbot Press 1918.

Dickinson, Page L., *The Dublin of Yesterday,* London: Methuen 1929.

Dunne, John J., *Streets Broad and Narrow,* Dublin: Helicon 1982.

Gillespie, Elgy, *The Liberties of Dublin,* Dublin: O'Brien Press 1973.

Gorham, Maurice, *Ireland Yesterday,* New York: Avenel Books 1971.

Gorham, Maurice, *Dublin Yesterday,* London: Fitzhouse Books 1972.

Johnston, Máirín, *Around the Banks of Pimlico,* Dublin: Attic Press 1985.

Joyce, Weston St John, *The Neighbourhood of Dublin,* Dublin: M. H. Gill and Son 1939.

Kain, Richard, *Dublin,* Norman: University of Oklahoma Press 1962.

Kearns, Kevin C., *Georgian Dublin: Ireland's Imperilled Architectural Heritage,* London: David and Charles 1983.

Kearns, Kevin C., *Dublin's Vanishing Craftsmen,* Belfast: Appletree Press 1986.

Kearns, Kevin C., *Stoneybatter: Dublin's Inner-Urban Village,* Dublin: Glendale Press 1989.

Kearns, Kevin C., *Dublin Street Life and Lore: An Oral History,* Dublin: Glendale Press 1991.

Kearns, Kevin C., *Dublin Tenement Life: An Oral History,* Dublin: Gill and Macmillan 1994.

Kearns, Kevin C., *Dublin Pub Life and Lore: An Oral History,* Dublin: Gill and Macmillan 1996.

Kearns, Kevin C., *Dublin Voices: An Oral Folk History,* Dublin: Gill and Macmillan 1998.

Kelly, Bill, *Me Darlin' Dublin's Dead and Gone,* Dublin: Ward River Press 1983.

Kelly, Deirdre, *Hands Off Dublin,* Dublin: O'Brien Press 1976.

Kennedy, Tom (ed.), *Victorian Dublin,* Dublin: Albertine Kennedy Publishers 1980.

Lehane, Brendan, *Dublin,* Amsterdam: Time-Life Books 1978.

Longford, Christine, *A Biography of Dublin,* London: Methuen 1936.

McDonald, Frank, *The Destruction of Dublin,* Dublin: Gill and Macmillan 1985.

Mac Tomáis, Éamonn, *Janey Mack, Me Shirt is Black,* Dublin: O'Brien Press 1974.

Mac Tomáis, Éamonn, *Gur Cakes and Coal Blocks,* Dublin: O'Brien Press 1976.

Morris, G. Ivan, *In Dublin's Fair City,* London: Home and Van Thal Ltd, 1947.

Neary, Bernard, *North of the Liffey,* Dublin: Lenhar Publications 1984.

Nolan, J., *Changing Faces,* Dublin: Elo Press 1982.

O'Brien, Joseph V., *Dear, Dirty Dublin,* Berkeley: University of California Press 1982.

O'Donovan, John, *Life by the Liffey,* Dublin: Gill and Macmillan 1986.

O'Keeffe, Phil, *Down Cobbled Streets: A Liberties Childhood,* Dingle: Brandon Press 1995.

Peter, A., *Sketches of Old Dublin,* Dublin: Sealy, Bryers and Walker 1907.

Peter, A., *Dublin Fragments,* Dublin: Hodges, Figgis and Company 1925.

Redmond, Lar, *Show Us the Moon,* Dingle: Brandon Books 1988.

Robertson, Olivia, *Dublin Phoenix,* London: Alden Press 1957.

St John, Pete, *Jaysus Wept!,* Birr: Midland Tribune 1984.

Sheehan, Ronan, and Walsh, Brendan, *The Heart of the City,* Dingle: Brandon Books 1988.

Somerville-Large, Peter, *Dublin,* London: Hamish Hamilton 1979.